THE WALL ST

OF INSTAGRAM
MARKETING

How to build your 100k+ IG Business Empire

VENN OPUTA

The Wall STREET OF INSTAGRAM MARKETING

How To Build Your 100k+ Instagram Business Empire

Venn Oputa

COPYRIGHT

DEDICATION

To my dad, who helped inspire me to become an entrepreneur through is life.

To my mom, who always knew my true worth and never stopped believing in me.

ACKNOWLEDGEMENT

There are so many people I want to thank for being with me through this journey.

Ideas that ultimately became the strategies behind everything inside of this book. I also want to thank my team—all the people who helped me to implement these ideas, put it down into writing and getting it ready to be published.

I can't mention everyone but here are to the few in no particular order:

Felix Ogbeide, Fola Opebiyi, Rotimi Tjani, Onakoya Adegbemi, Amidu Ololade and so many other people who played an immense role in getting this book ready.

Table of Contents

CHAPTER ONE

INTRODUCTION

In today's world of business, if you snooze, you lose! Over the decades, daily business transactions have shifted from traditional brick and mortar stores to online media. Staying updated on your way to harnessing leverage in the world of business is vital and when we discuss trends, social media is the go-to.

According to Forbes, as of January 2019, about forty-five percent of the world population makes use of social media. As of May 2019, total worldwide population was 7.7 billion, thus the internet has 4.4 billion users and there are 3.499 billion active social media users.

Thankfully, the world we live in today offers various tools with which one can grow their business and sell their products without having to shove it into people's hands at every bus stop, and social media happens to be one of the most easily accessible platforms to use.

The average daily time spent on social is 142 minutes and the majority of this time is used by people on social media; to keep up with online gossip or snoop on people or just while away time -- and that can be fun too -- but the hard truth is that none of those things can add any real value to one's life. As a matter of fact, social media can be just as much an entertainment medium as it can be a tool for serious business. You just need to know where to look and what to do. If you play your cards right, you'll be able to do more than just watch skits of people trying too hard to be funny or read comments of people trying too hard to be savage.

Don't get me wrong, there's a lot of fun stuff on social media, and everyone likes a good laugh, but there comes a time when you begin to wonder if you could do something more profitable with all that data.

When social media first came into our consciousness, it was mostly a tool for connecting with friends and family and making some new friends too. Before long, it additionally morphed into a tool for entertainment, and as people like to be amused, it drew interest from yet more users. These days, it's more like a tool for promoting businesses, amongst other things.

With platforms like Facebook receiving over two billion monthly visitors, Instagram holding its own quite well at one billion visitors monthly, and platforms like YouTube, Messenger, Twitter, LinkedIn, and several others boasting quite a sizeable audience, social media now boasts a bigger audience than all other traditional media put together.

With such a large audience comes ample opportunities to grow businesses. No wonder even the world's biggest brands are cutting down on their advertising budget in traditional media and channeling more money into social media in recent times. According to Vox, social media advertisers were expected to outspend TV advertisers by $40 billion in 2018. That meant that 40 percent of the world's ad spending was expected to take place online. It is a testament to the amount of clout social media has garnered in the last few years, and I could have learned this the hard way if I hadn't taken the right steps at the right time.

How It All Began...

I had a small startup that sold and distributed quality fabrics. Like most startups, we couldn't exactly get our hands on a lot of money. This meant that our marketing budget was very limited. The business was not booming as expected, and we were not making enough sales. Salaries were owed, and I could see the handwriting on the wall -- one that read something like the business was going to sink and there wasn't going to be any last-minute resuscitation.

At some point, I had only two options; throw in the towel and walk away or have one last big stab at it. Well, I opted for the latter, and that led me to discover things I didn't even know existed in the first place. That decision opened up a whole new world of possibilities to me, things I wasn't even looking for in the first place.

So, how did it happen, and what did I do exactly?

For starters, I resolved to make do with what I had and make things better. This first decision is actually very critical as all the secrets that will be subsequently revealed in this work will not help much if there isn't a conscious decision on your part to move things from where they are to where you want them to be.

I started with the tools I had. The startup I worked for was strictly an online store for fabrics and the reason we were struggling was that our products just weren't being seen by many people or weren't getting seen by the right eyes. In other words, our reach sucked. How much can you sell if you can't even get people's attention? Sure, you could have a fantastic product, even the best there is, but if you can't put it in front of the right audience, you'll be struggling to keep the lights on pretty soon. There is a possibility that your business will be outdone by competitors with far fewer quality products if they are able to amass a larger targeted following on social media.

So, I narrowed the root cause of our problem down to the fact that we weren't '*talking*' to a sizeable targeted audience. Our circle was small, and the bulk of the people in that circle didn't really care for what we were serving. We needed to talk to a lot more people who actually cared about what we sold. That was the only way we could have a reasonable shot at distributing our products, making sales, and staying in business.

Well, you know what they say; identifying a problem might be easy, solving the problem might be the tough nut to crack. As for me, I knew I wanted to make more sales, knowing how to use social media to achieve that wasn't what I was familiar with. It took some dedicated efforts, but I eventually figured it out and then I got the hang of it.

A good place to start when you don't know how to do what you want to do is knowing what you **don't** want to do. And I knew I didn't want to spread myself thin by trying to do so many different things at once. My company sold its products via a number of social media platforms with varying degrees of success (if we can call it that), and it had become obvious that some platforms did better than others when it came to our kind of business.

Twitter Just Didn't Fit

Looking at Twitter, I saw a lot of conversations and information exchange amongst intellectuals and plenty of talk from technocrats. Twitter also happens to be one of those few areas where people actually care more about what you have to say than what you've come to show them. Some say it's not for the soft-hearted or the dim-witted. Some less kind ones call it the nerdiest of all social media platforms.

Currently, with over 300 million active monthly, it's doing good numbers in terms of audience and reach, but it doesn't do so well as a visual medium. And given that selling products online requires a great deal of work on visuals (people are easily moved by what they see than what they hear or read), Twitter was never going to do justice to my quest.

Don't get me wrong; I love Twitter. In fact, there are those who say it is Twitter that makes other social media platforms interesting by sparking viral trends and starting conversations. However, the truth is that it is just hard to sell things on Twitter, especially those things whose sales heavily depend on visual appeals, like fabrics, for example. It just wasn't the right place to drive engagement and that was why I ruled out Twitter. I'd recommend using twitter for information related businesses like online publications or/and where you can respond to customer/client complaints.

Facebook Had Its Issues

The next option was Facebook, which was actually a better bet than Twitter, considering what we were looking to achieve. Twitter's loss was Facebook's gain. Where Twitter failed, Facebook triumphed. But it came with its own fair share of problems too.

Facebook remains the most-used social media platform in Nigeria (just like in many other places), and it was definitely going to get us the engagement and reach we sought. Plus Facebook was big on visuals and less talk, so it seemed to check a lot of boxes on the right side. So, we did try out Facebook for a while, up until Zuckerberg and the gang began to modify the way things worked.

On Facebook, you have to run paid ads for your products to get seen, even by your Facebook followers... A good amount of money went down the drain here since a few views and clicks on your product didn't always translate into purchases. So, in a way, we are sinking deeper with Facebook by spending money we didn't really have in the name of running ads.

Instagram It Is!

Instagram became the last resort. Actually, it was the final bet. If Instagram didn't work, it was a bust for us all. And boy, how did it work! Of all the social media platforms in existence, Instagram is perhaps the best bet when it comes to business. And that is because of its high affinity for visuals. Most people who are active on Instagram are mostly concerned about "*what they see*" more than anything else. That is to say; people frequent Instagram mostly to feed their eyes and amuse themselves, and not to work their minds or start up conversations.

Plus, it was far easier to cultivate a following and build engagement on Instagram than anywhere else. That's because customers are always looking for new images and interesting content with which they can while away time. Instagram excels at this. It is true that Twitter sets trends, but Instagram makes it go viral rather quickly with its mostly "fun-seeking" user base. Facebook is always the last to get in on trends.

Thus, Instagram proved the ideal platform to grow our brand and having narrowed it down; the next step was to play our cards right by putting most of our efforts on Instagram marketing. Not that we really had a good idea how to go about it at first, but, at least, now we know exactly what we wanted to do.

In between consuming volumes of online literature and watching YouTube videos with rapt attention, I had learned very little. The truth is that you can't find one consummate material that will unlock all the secrets of Instagram marketing, and I learned this the hard way.

I was too busy trying to consume every single bit of information there was, that I lost sight of one very fundamental detail that governs the art of taking on a new undertaking; actually, getting started. By the time I realized I couldn't possibly have figured it all out before starting out, I had lost precious time.

This brings me to my next statement; none of the strategies revealed in this book will make any difference if you don't actually **"do"** something. There are tons of materials out there, but none of those materials can teach you absolutely everything. They can only give you an idea at best. Much of the work involved in leveraging Instagram as a marketing tool is practical, so don't bury yourself in literature. This work is more like a guide that will help get you there faster, and nothing will change if you do not actually practice some of the provisions contained here.

Through trial and error, spraying, praying, and testing and tweaking over several years, I have been able to come up with something of a winning formula for Instagram marketing and this book is about sharing those insights with emphasis on **"practice, practice, and more practice**."

In this book, I will be sharing with you how I've been able to build Instagram marketing influencer pages that helped propel brands and create products that generated millions in revenue. Yes, I didn't do it for just my brand. I've gotten so good at it that I've been hired by several organizations to create successful Instagram pages. Trust me; it's a lucrative and exciting adventure.

Here, I am going to share all the insight from what we did right, the mistakes we made, and how we were able to leverage on our followers. If you go through the rest of the chapters, you will gain more insights so please don't miss any chapters as we will be discussing all you need to help you grow gradually, in order for you to experience and equip yourself with everything you need to be a successful as an Instagram marketer.

CHAPTER TWO

THE INSTAGRAM JOURNEY

First Steps: As I previously mentioned, I started out as a business owner selling fabrics on Instagram and Facebook. But I switched to Instagram entirely when I couldn't keep up with the cost of running ads and the unpredictability of the audience on Facebook. Instagram became something of a no-brainer for a variety of reasons. Instagram had credibility since it was favored by celebrities and other famous people in my country, and Facebook had become notorious for con men masquerading as who they aren't and defrauding people.

That's pretty much why people are still skeptical about patronizing online stores -- it's the fear of being swindled that discourages them. Even big e-commerce platforms like Jumia are having a hard time convincing people to buy stuff online, which is why they leverage on the option of pay-on-delivery to help boost trust; something that takes away from the fundamental idea of online commerce. In my country, there is a trust deficit that bedevils anything that has something to do with buying goods and services online. Whether it's the fear of being conned out of their hard-earned money or not getting exactly what they paid for, individuals always have lots of reasons to not want to try out online purchases.

But Instagram gives something no other platform can quite give; something called credibility. If you are credible enough, people will have no second thoughts about buying what you are selling. Therefore, many celebrities who became famous through movies and music are gradually branching into sales of their own products and at crazy prices too, even if some of those products are actually worthwhile.

That's the power of credibility. It makes it very easy to influence people's purchasing habits, and that is why a person that had the opportunity of living with 19 other people in a popular reality TV Show that aired for three months can sell out 24 hours after launching her clothing line! But we can't all be famous, can we? We absolutely can't all be celebrities. Although the good news is that being a celebrity is not the only way to build credibility! At least, that's true for Instagram. There is another kind of credibility that comes from the number of followers. The higher your number of followers on Instagram, the more your social proof and social currency. With more followers, people are more disposed to trust you and more willing to patronize you.

This is actually where the work begins -- amassing a following that will make you a lot more credible. Some of the time, it's not about people not seeing your product. It's usually about people taking a pass on your product mostly because they don't know who you are... The fact that you do not have a lot of followers can only discourage them. So the first lesson I had to master with regards to Instagram marketing was building a following. And thankfully, I became pretty good at it that I was able to grow my page, promote my business, and even secure lucrative offers from clients who wanted me to handle their social media pages. This book is all about walking you through the process.

How I Grew An Instagram Following

Even though I sound like I have it all figured out -- and I probably do, at least, in these circles -- I didn't exactly get off on the right foot. There were many mistakes here and there, but I saw it all as an experiment to determine what works and what doesn't. (That's how I was able to get through those days when I didn't get as many hits as I thought I would).

The first thing that courted my curiosity was how people with multiple accounts have a huge number of followers and were able to grow those pages. Managing one page was hard enough, and the fact that there were people who were winning at managing multiple pages made me wonder. But I knew it couldn't have been rocket science. For the very fact, that it was being handled by actual people, I knew I could do it too if I tried hard enough. If anything, those people just knew what I didn't know, and I didn't know because I hadn't learned. So, I began to do a lot of background research. The thing is, I tend to be pedantic, and when I dove into the research, I may have gotten carried away. I feel like I researched a little too much, but you know what they say about no knowledge going to waste.

After sitting through hours of YouTube videos and Instagram courses on Udemy and many others, I have come to realize that, at their very best, these resources only offered a shallow insight on how to grow followers on Instagram. But here are some of the routes through which you can grow followers on Instagram, and note that some are more effective than others.

Strategies For Growing Instagram Followers

➢ The Follow and Unfollow Method

There is quirky saying around here which goes something like following being free of charge and followers being expensive. You can't really control the number of followers you get, especially when you are just starting out, but you sure can make the most of one thing you have control over; whom you choose to follow.

Just as its name implies, the follow and unfollow method does involve following and unfollowing. But just not the way most people know it. In Instagram marketing terms, the follow and unfollow method entails systematically following popular persons in your niche, and the following the followers of those people and then unfollowing in a controlled manner after a while.

Let's say you were selling fabrics like I was, using this method would mean following wedding and fashion pages, as well as the most active persons on those pages. You can identify the most active persons on a particular page by switching on notifications for that page and taking note of the first people to always comment on a post on that page. You can follow them and start mirroring the pages such people seem interested in until they start following you and you unfollow them after a while. I'm talking about no less than 500 follows. That's usually a good place to start.

But the problem with this method is that it is inherently slow. It takes a lot of time. It's kind of a long shot, and if you're not a very patient person, you might begin to feel like you are not doing anything. I realized this, and so I dove deeper for other methods, and I did find some other interesting ones.

➤ The Power Like Method

Have you ever wondered how some of the people you follow reach the Explore page over and over again? Want to have your Instagram posts go viral also? Well, with Power Likes, - you can. Power likes are likes from an Instagram account with a substantial following, including verified accounts. When an account with a large following and high engagement likes your post, your post will show up on the explore page, which consists of their followers.

When your post receives likes from multiple profile accounts, it will be recognized as a "top-performing post." A high-performing post is a post with very high engagement, strengthening your chances of appearing on the Explore page. With likes coming in minutes, Instagram is under the impression that the post is starting to go viral due to the speed of exposure and how popular it has become amongst a large number of users.

People use power likes to circumvent the "*natural*" process of landing followers and organic impressions on your page. They pay a certain amount of money to influential personalities who already have a huge following to like their post and even comment on it for good measure.

Power likes can do a good job of improving the visibility of the content of your page, reaching a wider audience. It's like getting an endorsement from an established individual with the hope that it will attract people to what you are offering. And many times it does. Though nothing is certain. Nothing beats organic engagement, and you might need to use power likes again and again, such that it becomes the only way your post can actually get the engagement you need. It's like an athlete using a particular drug over and over again to boost performance, without which they are powerless. In the long run, it will haunt your business. But if done right, and with some luck on your side, power likes can actually be a winner.

> ➢ Using Viral Content

One of the biggest mistakes I made initially was to fixate on what I had come to sell. On Instagram, nobody really cares about what you've come to sell until you draw their attention to it.

At first, I was so engrossed in putting my fabrics out there. I had some really good stuff, alright, but I terribly miscalculated how people would react to it. If you're trying to build a business on Instagram, you'll be making a terrible move if you think you can rely on the "awesomeness' of what you've come to sell.

Granted, you might actually have the best quality products, but nobody will give you the attention you desire if you don't give them a reason to. You'll give them a reason to care about what your business is if they trust you. They'll trust you if you have credibility. You'll have credibility if you have the following. Now you won't get that following if all you do is post pictures of the nice handmade shoes you sell or the handwoven handbags you import from Ethiopia. You're going to have plenty of time to post your product, so don't jump into it. Take the time to explore viral content. And there's plenty of it on Instagram. Viral content is those ones that everyone is raving about on Instagram.

It could be a comedy skit, a music rendition, an awkward moment caught on camera, or unbelievable footage from an amazing moment - the internet never seems to run out of those. You'll be amazed at how fast your page can grow if you have a lot of cool, viral content on it. Just don't forget to give reference to the source of the content, or you can just tag the original owner of the post. I shall be revisiting how you can go about growing your business page with viral content in the latter part of this work. Until then, just bear in mind that parts of growing your business on Instagram might involve not doing your business at all!

How To Go About Growing Your Page

Once I began to study the pages of people and businesses that were doing quite well on Instagram, one particular trend jumped right at me.

I discovered that those accounts with a considerable number of followers had one thing in common; besides their actual business, they also **posted a lot of viral content**. They did post a lot of their stuff, but they also posted a lot of viral content.

These are people that were doing great in business. It was quite telling that such individuals recognized that marketing isn't just about them, and that's a fact. At the end of the day, marketing isn't just about you and what you've come to sell. At the end of the day, people care about what they like and not just what you like. So, as some politicians would say, you've got to give the people what they like to get what you want.

Giving the people what they want in this context means deviating somewhat from the real business you have and gripping the attention of a wider audience with some interesting content that has the potential to go viral. Thankfully, there are a lot of pages on Instagram from where you can get those sorts of things that can move people. Just be sure to give link backs to the original sources of whatever you are reposting on your page.

After I noticed how those guys managed to incorporate viral content into their business content, I started to try out some of the patterns I had recognized on the two Instagram accounts I had going on (fabrics and weddings). I started by looking at accounts with a good number of likes and videos that were doing similar stuff, pages that were doing okay with the sales of similar products and I tried to make out what was working for them.

Once I had found the best performing contents, I took note of them with the hashtags used on those posts. It hit me that those folks really did take their time to find really good content, and the truth is that it was easy getting quality content and giving them mentions in the posts. I had to be consistent, and I had to be picky with the content - there's a lot of stuff out there, you just have to make out the really good ones. Those are the ones that will get you the views, and then the likes, and then, the follows. One important lesson I learned from all this was something I like to call the three C's - content, captions, and call to action, which we shall now look at it in some detail.

Content is everything on Instagram, and not just Instagram, media business in general. It's a battle for the eyeballs. Okay, not literally, but a battle still. Social media is a relatively new arm of the media business, but just like its older cousins; TV, radio, and newspapers, it's all about who gets the most attention from the audience.... Now, you can't get the attention of the audience (the eyeballs) if you are not putting out great content out there. Content is king in this business. The bulk of the audience always gravitates towards the platform with the coolest content!

Even in the mainstream media business, it's all about who's got more of the good stuff. Nobody wants to check out any platform with shitty content. If you have a knack for identifying content with the potential to go viral, you are already halfway through the journey. Think of content as the building blocks of your online presence. The type of posts you upload, and the timeliness of those posts can do a great job for your page. You can start by identifying those pages with the good stuff. Then do your work around trying to mirror those pages. I shall go deeper into how to make content work for you subsequently

Caption. Print media folks place a premium on the title of their content because it often proves the difference between going through a post or simply passing upon it. It's pretty much the same idea when it comes to social media captions. They work the same way as titles in articles.

Even as it is important to have great content, all that effort could go down the drain if you don't pay attention to your captions. The content could be great, alright, but if you don't accompany that content with the magic words, you might not get the engagement you'd have gotten if you took the time out to flavor your post with the right words.

Captions are the cheeky lines that should accompany your posts on Instagram. You will usually find it at the bottom of Instagram posts, and if you are familiar with the app, you'd know that you inadvertently look at captions every single time you scroll through your feed and those captions help you decide if you really want to spend time on that post or just scroll past. All these usually happen in a split second, and that is why it can seem like nothing, but it's actually a biggie.

Great captions make even the shittiest content seem like good stuff. Captions can be used as bait to keep people attached to your content even though they would rather not. The goal is to get people's attention, and you don't want to leave anything to chance. Your content must be followed with excellent captions to get more hits and clicks. This is what drives engagement.

In many ways, this is the business end of things. It is the whole point of doing any of this. This is the part where you inspire action from the viewers of your post. So, you've done your homework, your content is great, and captions are on point. Now, what? Well, this is where you tell people exactly what you'd like them to do.

You have to be clear about it -- do you want people to buy your product, do you want them to follow your page, or would you like them to click on a link on your bio? You can spell it out clearly.

When you are just starting out, the clever move will be to tell your audience to follow your page, and they will if you get your content and captions right. There was this one time I was working on the fan page of an upcoming artist. What I did was to post viral content of people dancing and singing, something related to his venture. I followed those posts up with great captions and call-to-action for people to follow the artist. For something so basic, it gave the artist over 30% growth on their personal page.

The play-by-play of how it all came together will be discussed soon. It's the same strategy I used on all my Instagram pages and the results were tremendous. Those pages grew at quite a pace and I was able to replicate the same tactics over and over with similar results.

So, in summary, the idea is to consistently crowd your page with viral post after viral post. Then, following those up with some really nice captions and a clear call-to-action. One viral post could give about a thousand followers in the span of three days. So, imagine you are able to post 3 to 4 viral contents in a day, with the right caption and call-to-action. Do the math on how many followers you might be able to get in a month.

CHAPTER THREE

The Play-By-Play On How To Get It Done

I'd like to spell something out clearly -- Instagram marketing is NOT a part-time job. It's not something you trivialize by putting it on the side for later. If anything, it demands even more seriousness, commitment, and consistency than a regular job would.

I'm talking about a full-on commitment that involves working more hours than you would in a regular job. So, it's not going to work out for you if you're going to go at it like some kind of side hustle. So let's get started.

Once you have identified a particular page that you are trying to model, or perhaps a business page that has grown its following into the level that you are seeking, start by turning on your notification for that particular page. Take note of the frequency of their posts. The goal is to have an idea of how many times they post in a day. That should be your target.

What I actually did was to make a list of all the people that were selling the same thing I was offering. Just like any other business, sometimes to move ahead, you have to keep an eye on what the competition is doing. There are those who have been there and done that and to get ahead, you just have to follow in their footsteps -- no need to reinvent the wheel.

Leverage On Testimonials

From the list of competitors, I noticed that most product selling Instagram pages usually add visuals that portray how the product actually looks on people or the marvelous results the product has produced in people.

There are no two ways about it -- when you see how a product looks so good on other people, or how well it worked for them, it is only natural that you'd want the same for yourself, and this is what successful Instagram pages leverage on.

By showcasing their products, they create awareness and a desire among followers, encouraging them to buy the product or pay for the service. Business handling services tend to put up testimonies about how their services were able to achieve amazing results in satisfied clients. I began to notice these patterns. This was kind of different from growth hacking which involved viral content, and the three C's that have been discussed earlier.

The pattern of coming up with testimonials of people or previous customers that were happy with the products and services was a notable take-home. Some went as far as faking the testimonies or getting friends and families to give great reviews. They posted all these on their page, and it did them a solid.

Posting testimonials on your page has the effect of attracting other potential clients and making them want to try out the products or services. Brands use this to create a desire in the customer. They do this by posting their product alongside something interesting like testimonials. This helped me set up Instagram pages that seemed very trustworthy.

Use Power Likes To Your Advantage

As mentioned earlier, power likes are likes that come from "big' Instagram accounts. You can think of big Instagram accounts as those that belong to established influencers or some hugely-followed celebrity.

People often buy power likes from big accounts or celebrities. If your posts get engagement from big accounts, Instagram algorithms work such that your post is pushed to the top. That's also how you get into the Explore page.

Power likes can give you a wider audience and put your product in front of a lot of people. That can give you a lot more engagement and a lot more followers. Essentially this would mean more customers for your business. More so, the celebrity-endorsement look that comes with power likes is a good look for your business. People generally have confidence in products and/or services that have passed the "*celebrity test*." That is, an okay from a prominent person generally puts people at ease when it comes to doing business with you.

From my experience, though, I wouldn't always advise people to buy power likes. With the right taglines and viral content, big accounts will engage your post, and that is an organic power-like. Get it right from your own end, and you won't have to part with money you don't really have to get what you are not even certain of.

Do your posting pace, and it will be worth it. There are a lot of tools that I have also tried out, and they are very effective. There is Google Nitro; it used to come with a 30-day free trial, but these days, it's just 14 days. I have made use of this app to get new accounts started and gain followers with viral content, great captions, and hashtags.

There is another tool I also tried, and I recommend it. It's called InstaSuit, which is a beneficial program used to boost Instagram accounts using the follow and unfollow method. This can help you get a head start before you get the hang of leveraging viral posts from popular accounts.

Mine is quite a simple story, and a lot of it has the theme of consistency and hard work. The truth is that all of this wouldn't have been possible if I didn't take action. So you have to take action. If you read this book and don't take action, you are not going to see results. The pages of this book won't magically start to help you gain so many followers and engagement without acting.

If you follow some of the techniques described in this book and be consistent, you will experience growth, and that is what this book is all about, to help people see that it is really possible to have millions of followers if they follow through and stick to the plan.

You Need To Be SMART With Instagram Marketing

For the utmost results, you need to have smart social media marketing goals. We need to know the appropriate time to use certain strategies and when to stop using them. Sometimes, we often fail at following through with certain strategies because our goals are simply too vague, unplanned, and unrealistic. Achieving a realistic goal with certain strategies can make you feel strong and well-organized, which often leads to following through on more positive outcomes. So what makes the difference between success and failure? It all comes down to being

SMART: Specific, Measurable, Action-Oriented, Realistic and Timed. This five-step method of goal setting is a valuable tool when trying to set realistic and attainable goals, and will set you up for a successful outcome.

SPECIFIC: This means that every goal should be clearly defined. For example, planning to ensure you sell certain amounts of products via social media is not a specific goal. Rather knowing the number of active followers, you need on your page to achieve that level of sales is more specific. So, let's say with active 10,000 followers you will be able to make an average of 500 sales on every product you introduce on your page.

MEASURABLE: This means that you should be able to clearly measure your progress. Saying *"I want a million followers"* gives you no clear way to assess your progress. In order to re-frame the above goal so that it is measurable, start by understanding your knowledge base about what it will take to have a million followers. Then, determine daily steps to take in order to achieve the overall goal. For example, if you post five times daily and get an average of 20,000 reaches, probably 500 profiles visits, and about 200 hundred followers. With that, you can estimate that the amount of viral posts you will probably require to get about 10,000 active followers.

ACTION-ORIENTED: This means you should outline specific steps that will enable you to successfully complete your goal. "*I want to be able to post five contents per day*" is a good starting place but does not include any action details. Instead, you should say: "*Per day, I want to be able to post five engaging contents. I will achieve this goal by searching and organizing content a day before. One post every four hours*".

REALISTIC: When it comes to marketing your products on Instagram, we all tend to want the unrealistic and a typically quick fix. Don't let yourself fall into this trap by setting unattainable goals such as wanting a million followers overnight. Instead, aim to get a thousand followers per week. Attempting to gain followers faster than this is unrealistic and will only set you up for disappointment.

TIMED: This means you should set deadlines that will keep you on track. Set a firm date for that target, and then establish mini-goal deadlines between now and your targeted date so you have plenty of time to achieve your final goal. If you track your progress with mini-goals over the course of that time, you won't be scrambling to see results before your targeted time. It must be a gradual continuous process.

CHAPTER FOUR

INSTAGRAM STRATEGIES

Instagram strategies are simple moves that can help you grow your page, those things that can make your brand more visible. And there are quite a number of them. Granted, you've come to sell your product, you've come to talk people into accepting that you've got something they need, but you'll achieve the direct opposite of that if you just try to shove it down their throats.

Marketing Isn't Just About You

One thing you should have at heart when trying to market something on Instagram is the fact that you have got to give the people what they want to get some of what you need. You have got to understand that marketing isn't about you. If you're just starting out Instagram, it's a wrong move to just jump right into it and bamboozle people with your product. We get it, you have the finest quality hair care product, but nobody wants to see that all the time. You'll just be putting people off if you just show up from nowhere and be all over the place with posts centered on your product. It's a sure way to go under as a fresher in the game.

The wise move would be to take advantage of the prime niches -- areas that people are always naturally drawn towards. Areas like entertainment, comedy, music, fashion, style, luxury, entrepreneurship, and viral clips normally get a lot of attention on Instagram. So, use it to your advantage. Your own original content might not go viral, but contents from these pages are viral.

If you are interested in entrepreneurship, for example, the prudent move would be to create another page that motivates entrepreneurs. You can name this page after a popular entrepreneur, a millionaire, or a renowned business mentor.

Such a motivational page built upon the image of an accomplished entrepreneur can amass millions of followers with well-selected motivational content, good captions, clear call to action, and the appropriate tag linking this motivational page to their own personal or business account.

If you are into fashion, start a styles page. The styles pages will go viral before your main page can go viral. Just like my company, we started with @fabricsphere -- our main pages on which we market our products. Then, we created two other pages, @fabricsphereweddings, and @asoebifabricsphere, where we post viral content, which increases our likelihood of engagement and follows. These other accounts were more like a viral post page where we post viral content about weddings, styles, and lifestyles.

The growth of those pages was tremendous; it easily outpaced the growth of our main business page because they were fun pages. But that was the idea. We used this to our advantage by tagging our main account and dropping a call to action for people to follow our business page. And they did! With consistency, we recorded tremendous growth on our business page. This generated millions in revenue for us and grew our follower base on the main account organically.

I applied this same strategy in the entertainment niche when I was contracted to work on the page of an artist named @jaytrigga. He was an upcoming act, so I knew it'd be difficult to get people to care. Instead,

I leveraged a more popular, fast-rising act known as Teni Makanaki. I created a fan page account for him called @tenietriggafans. We had fused his brand with a fast-growing artist in Nigeria and posted contents that were peculiar to both of them.

This fan page account grew very fast and was then used to influence the artist's main account. There are several places to get viral contents to help grow these influencer accounts. In total, we created four fan page accounts that grew exponentially, and all four fan page accounts were used to feed the main account. This grew the artist's account very fast, giving a wider audience, which is always good for an upcoming act.

The technique is about creating your own influencer page where you post content that has gone viral with good hashtags. Then, you ask followers on that influencer page to follow your main account. This method works so well if you want to grow organic followers that can easily convert to buys of your product and services. So find a niche that people care about and attach it to your brand. It works like magic — every single time.

How Successful Accounts Do It

For the strategy highlighted above, Instagram firstly shows your content to your followers before it is then viewed by a wider audience. For that first one hour, you need a post that will connect really well with your audience. If it connects well enough with your audience, it will be passed over to a wider audience.

After listing out competitors, I would go through their pages, view their comments, and then follow and message people that were interested in the same product. I will engage anyone that is interested in the same product that my competitor is selling.

Start by listing all the influencers and competitors in your niche. Follow all of them and switch on notifications. Take note of how frequently they post and the first responders to their posts.

Those first people that post on your competitor's page are those you should engage in. Follow them and send them messages. Follow users that engage on your competitor's post in an hour; this gives you a high percentage of engaging people.

We discovered that whatever our competitors were doing right, we needed to model after that. You then need to make sure that your content, and product, and services, are better than that of your competitors. This gives you a level playing field. This is the first step into getting your first 1000 followers and buyers.

If you have a thousand followers and you can convince just 10% of them to buy a product at 30 percent markup, then you will be making up a lot of revenue from that few.

This can be somewhat tough initially, but it is better to start that way. As time goes on, with the use of some software that I will be discussing later, it gets easier. Sometimes, you need to automate these processes, so you don't always have to be awake and manually doing everything by yourself. With the use of software like Goldnitro, Instazood, and Jarvee, you can catch a break while resting in the knowledge that your work is being done and your strategy is being followed through.

There is a follow and unfollow method, which is a precise targeting method. You are not just following and unfollowing random pages; you are following people that already follow some of your competitors that are doing very well. You switch on their notification and those followers that comment within the first hour on your competitor's page. These are the active followers/buyers, which will form most of the first 1000 followers that you need to get started.

These are some of the strategies used by successful pages, that have varying degrees of success and different speeds of achievement. Some of the strategies yield results that are more telling than others, but the ever-present term is **consistency**.

Strategies mean nothing without consistency. It begins with a firm resolve to keep at it. Even with the best tools at your disposal, it will amount to nothing if you are not consistent and intentional about your actions. So, whether you want to use the follow and unfollow method, the power like method, or the fan page method, you just have to keep going at it.

A good rule of thumb is to see to it that you're constantly doing the most and you're putting out enough viral content out there. If your competitors are doing eight posts daily, try to top that. That's how you know you are doing the most.

Leverage Instagram Stories and Highlights

Today, you probably won't get through any sort of Instagram-related advice or tutorial without a mention of Instagram stories. Instagram recently reported that stories have up to 400 million (yes, 400 million!) daily active users. That means Instagram stories have twice as many users as Snapchat. There's a huge audience here—making it a good place to promote your products and make some sales.

How? With the sense of urgency that Instagram stories inspire (since they disappear after 24 hours!), you can use them to give a heads up about a current sale or promo code. That will inspire users to head on over and buy something. Instagram also has story highlights, which allows you to save certain clips in a category that appears at the top of your profile.

Whether you're providing a demonstration, talking about sizing, or giving a sneak peek at an upcoming product launch, your Instagram story highlights are the perfect place to gain more interest in your products. Users can access those clips at any time in order to get the lowdown on the products they're most interested in.

That all helps to get your products in front of more eyeballs. But, what about actually making the sale? Brands who have made the switch to a business profile and have more than 10,000 followers can add "swipe up" links directly to their stories. When users swipe up as instructed, they're brought directly to the product page to get more information and make a purchase.

In short, don't neglect Instagram Stories as part of your Instagram marketing strategy. They're highly engaging and an effective way to drive more interest in your products.

Encouraging Fan Participation

It's all about engagement. Are you groaning? I know—you've heard it a million times, but it's true. Learning how to sell on Instagram is a group activity whether you like it or not!

Here's the thing, though; While a high level of engagement is necessary to make a sale, getting that level of commitment from your followers isn't easy. In fact, it's pretty challenging most of the time. This is why you need to incentivize them. You need to give them a reason to interact and ultimately purchase.

In reality, incentivizing a sale can be as simple as offering a limited-time promo code. Followers who were previously on the fence about ordering will feel more motivated to buy when they feel like they need to snag a discount before it goes away.

But, while blasting out a promo code might lead to a brief uptick in sales, it doesn't really do much in terms of your engagement. Here's where giveaways and contests come in. You encourage engagement on your posts as part of the contest, and then pick a winner from those participants.

For example, perhaps you'll post a contest photo that people need to comment on in order to enter for a chance to win one of your products for free. Not only are you skyrocketing your engagement on that one photo, but you're also (hopefully!) identifying some brand advocates.

When you choose your winner(s), encourage them to post a photo of themselves with their free product and tag you in it. They're spreading the word about your brand and products to their followers, which expands your reach beyond your existing audience. Plus, if that person happens to love their free product? Chances are, they'll come back to purchase more. You just gained a loyal customer and brand ambassador—for very little effort.

CHAPTER FIVE

THE THREE C's

Given what we discussed in the last chapter, by now getting 1000 followers should be a walk in the park. All you must do is make sure that the content you are posting or sharing on the page is highly engaging. Remember what they say about content being king. Most of the time, the importance of compelling content is overrated. What people do not realize is that the number of followers they have ultimately determines the kind of growth your business will experience in the long run. These people, at the very least, are the ones hitting the like button, commenting, sharing, and even buying products and services you are showcasing. So whatever you give to them must be organic. Not just that, but the content also must be well-targeted as well as **unique**.

Do whatever you want with your Instagram account, but never buy followers. If you do so, your account will suffer for it in the long run, as you will be left with a bunch of people who have no interest whatever in what you are offering. No matter the kind of services you are providing, never offer money to get followers in return - we are repeating this for the sake of emphasis. Rather than investing in such a thing that doesn't yield even 2 percent of the input, focus on the three Cs of Instagram businesses. They include Consistency, Content, and Caption. On the surface, they look like a trio of simple words you can attend with a wave of a hand and a spark of thought, but you may never know the interesting market results that lie beneath them.

CONSISTENCY

There aren't really any shortcuts when it comes to becoming a master at something. There is no such thing as waking up one day to recreate the Mona Lisa when you never have as much as painted a single picture in your life. Well, that is except you have been possessed overnight by the ghost of Leonardo Da Vinci himself. That's to say that all great things that happen in life require practice, patience, dedication, and most of all the hard work. Consistency is just about a very efficient umbrella for all four.

The same thing applies when it comes to marketing your business on Instagram or anywhere else for that matter. In the same way, one cannot expect the very first blog post one puts out there to go viral. One cannot immediately rake in millions of followers the first day one signs up on any social media platform. If you take today's world of digital marketing into keen consideration, you would realize that there is no strategic leeway or formula for instantaneous success. If you really desire long-term and sustainable growth, you need to take a consistent approach to whatever you do as regards to marketing.

In order to get this right and know the amount of consistency you need, check out your competitor's pages or influencer's pages and turn on their notification. You may discover that some of them post multiple times a day if someone at the post of your niche is posting about ten times a day you will want to come close to how much you have to post every day for you to replicate the same level of engagement. At least you must have a post every day. So be almost 70 percent as consistent as an influencer page. Find out influencers on your page, switch on notification and post as much time as they post. It's just like the news, for people addicted to the news, they know it's always going to come, so you must feed the audience. Don't starve your followers; your post is just like their food.

A Plan and A Calendar To Start

Businesses are not run under the wing of seraphim or with a steady stream of prayers. The same thing pretty much applies to marketing. You need to create some strategies, carve out time to do something about them and have a calendar that spells out the details of your immediate milestones and later steps in digital marketing. Before going live with a blog or committing some bucks for ad space, you need to take time to do meaningful research. Make dead sure you have an understanding of your target market, their buying habits, the best strategies for them, and how your enterprise fits into their manner of living.

From the hours of writing down stuff and looking for valuable information, you will be able to come up with the right strategies.

Strategizing, among many other things, involves creating the kind of content that attracts leads, improving the SEO of your website, relevantly and putting money into ad space. The moment you have been able to decide on what strategies you will use for your marketing, you can begin to plan out when and how often you are going to work on them.

Sorry to burst your bubble, but there is no such thing as spending a single weekend on your marketing and feeling it is going to be good enough to take you throughout the rest of the year. Because things never stop changing, especially digitally, you need always to be working to improve your strategies. Good marketing needs constant publishing, updating, and modifications. It does not matter how effective you think the ad published or article churned is. When it is three years old, it naturally becomes less converting. Once you begin a strategy, do everything possible within your power to make it to the finish line.

And You Need To Keep Up

Some businesses hire people to handle everything related to digital marketing, and even the same offline. If you do not have someone dedicated to this full time, then you might want to consider setting aside one day or more in a week to work on it, nothing else. This done, you will have just about enough time to churn out quality content, analyze your analytics and schedule when things should go live on your Instagram page. Here is some good news - you can keep producing new marketing and improving your tactics without having to let your business fall apart. There is always a balance that works for your business, so all you need do is find it. That way, you can continue growing without other important parts of the business being regrettably left out of the mix.

To really grow your business via digital marketing, you need to stick to a normal pattern of updating, uploading, and producing fresh content year on year. Have you ever heard of content marketing? Well, it's necessary. If you take time off, even if it's just one month, can result in unwanted turnarounds in online selling. Losing the momentum of improving your SEO is the least of it, as you will also fall behind your competitors. What's more, you will have to -unwillingly- let your current or returning customers go. Even when there are a lot of factors stopping you from doing it, you need to push yourself to never relent on your digital marketing.

Being On Top Of Re-evaluations And Changes

When we say you have to be consistent with what you do with your online business, we do not necessarily mean you should be doing the same thing over and over. You will agree very well to the reality that people change and that industries know how to adapt more than almost anything - and so does marketing. If you keep repeating the same approach every year, you will find yourself at the rear of the race eventually - like way behind. What is also possible is that the strategies you are currently using will not be as effective as they used to be, and that is one solid reason you have to look into some kind of experimentation.

One way to re-evaluate and make changes when and where necessary is to keep a watchful eye on the analytics of your website as well as other useful data that have to do with your campaigns. If you do not see the results from a specific approach, then you need to find out whether it was really worth the time and your dollars. Perhaps, there is a page that is not performing as well as it should. Now is the best time to experiment with it, try new stuff, carry out A/B tests, and learn all you can during the processes. Just as they would tell the website administrators who are looking to create the perfect landing pages, it takes several iterations to get the right one.

That's not all. You also need to keep your guard up regarding future trends for customer services and marketing. While doing this, think about how they will impact your business. Case in point, with all the media reports we are getting, there are rather too many signs that Artificial Intelligence (AI) will play quite a significant role in businesses of the coming years, and marketing is not left out. Chatbots could very well replace customer service, and AI may be able to assist us in identifying data trends and even help with social media interactions. Even though these are yet to materialize, as an online entrepreneur, you need to figure out how new trends could impact your industry and marketing early on.

Graphics, Imagery, And Tone Need To Be Consistent Too

The sort of branding and graphics you create for your business is a key identifier for your customers, in case you didn't know. Nevertheless, we see a brand using some unbranded graphics, most of which are pulled from stock image websites. What these people do not know is that this works against them, especially when they are trying to create a brand image that is instantly identifiable. The font, colors, and styles that appear on the stock images are more likely to be in dispute with the kind of features outlined in your branding guidelines. For this reason - and many others - your graphics need to be branded, identifiable and most of all, consistent.

In a similar way, images used outside of graphics need to have a consistent style that matches brand identity. This includes any kind of photography used on your digital channels. For example, if you are building a luxury brand, your images need to reflect this. They need to be high-end, sleek photos that speak volumes about your value to both potential and existing customers. Many online businesses do not keep their imagery consistent - they just post a Farago of high-quality images and poorly shot photos that could be blurry, out of focus, or not framed properly. This can go a long way in confusing your audience who expect a certain level of quality and consistency from the kind of content you produce. By all means possible, try to keep the imagery very consistent. Your lighting, framing, color schemes, and quality should always be in unison, in order to continue the goal of all your posts being instantly recognizable. If you have to hire a professional photographer or graphics designer to keep your images unanimous, do so - or go learn some things yourself.

The wording of your Instagram posts also needs to have a specific tone of voice that resounds throughout all of your work. Keep the practice of good spelling, grammar, and punctuation in order to remain professional. Depending on the nature of orientation of your target audience, you may want your writing style to be sleek and elegant, professional and informative, playful and down to earth, direct, and enlightening, or whichever tone you think to help you communicate your brand in the best way. The tone with which you start should be the one you continue using to communicate. You may confuse your audience if you start out as playful and down to earth only to switch to a direct approach a little later. You need to retain the tone that got you your customers in the first place.

CHAPTER SIX

CONTENT REMAINS KING

"Content is king" is a popular phrase used a marketing buzzword, and it only becomes more relevant year on year. In today's times when consumers are obviously demanding and more tech-savvy than ever, businesses have no choice than to step up their digital marketing game in order to attract, inspire, engage and convert their potential clients. They also need to do this to stay in the game. This goes to say that content will never stop being in the heart of marketing because no one can ever challenge the power of words. Truly the best and the most known efficient way to connect with any kind of audience, content helps you create brand awareness, showcase your brand's authority and help you build customer trust.

The powerful influence of content marketing can be recognized through a lot of realities. One of the most prominent examples is research which found that more than 90 businesses decided to turn to content marketing in 2016. More firms had their minds set on rubbing shoulders with content marketers to hop on the bandwagon and ride with the speedy digital world in the years to come. Simply said, there is no way to overemphasize or exaggerate while stating that every revenue-raking business you know today has pumped in some funds, time and effort into content marketing in order to scale up the tree of success. There is a heck load of reasons why content marketing will remain relevant to promoting any kind of business.

When using Instagram to grow your business, it is necessary to brick lay an audience that will always be engaged by your content and loyal to your brand. The thing is how then you can make sure these followers are attracted by your posts and in turn, help you grow as an Instagram business? I've got three words for you - Quality Instagram Content. Oh, you do not have time or perhaps resources to take your own photos for the business? No need to fret. There is a multiplicity of ways to create engaging feeds with cool aesthetics. That's possible even if you're pushing something not so glamorous, Tupperware for example. Or maybe you are promoting something that is completely digital, seemingly impossible to see and feel. Well, let's skip the wedding and go straight to the buffet - how can you create quality Instagram content?

Keep A Keen Eye On Templates

There is a cornucopia of tools out there tailored to help you create the most compelling and effective Instagram posts, and you do not have to be a savvy Photoshop person to use them. Online tools such as Spark Post - which was designed by Adobe - Canva, and Venngage really come in handy when you want to craft some mind-blowing visuals for your social media page. Or probably you need to create a post that promotes a specific offer. Maybe you want to announce the new opening times for your business and need a template to do so? Maybe not all of those - maybe there is a particular recipe you have shared on a beloved blog that you need to push.

The main point is, whatever message you intend on sending, there is a simple yet effective template to help you with it. When you want to boost your page for sales, you can go for some plain or pattern layout for a simplified look. There's even a product image as an alternative. If you have a war chest of high-resolution images of your products, it could really go a long way to help you wriggle from a tight situation, especially in cases when you run low on content to share on your page. A simple, slick photo of the product will work you something amazing for your engagement if you have a strong base of fans and followers.

High-Quality Stock Images

First off, stock images have been in some kind of bad wrap as of late, but that does not mean they cannot still be used. On the other hand, these images can be used to create a variety of feed when you use them in amalgamation with other images, and templates, for example. Having said that, you need to know that stock images actually have all the makings of what should be given a prime spot in your feed. But be wary of some of these guys, because not all of them are friendly. Some can be really terrible for your Instagram. There are places you can find high-quality images that do not have "stock" written all over them. Yes, that's true. Sites such as Unsplash or Stocksnap can really help, as they offer an extensive range of images for free, you also stand the chance of finding something that agrees well with your business niche.

Some people are willing to put some money down to get the right images going for them. If you are one of them, then that means you have a bit of a budget to spend on sites like Stocksy. As anyone would expect with a paid service, the quality of the pictures sold here is remarkably better, and they also offer a wide variety of options. The best advice is that you should make sure your purchases are for the correct sizes of the images. There are a few of them offered at different prices. When buying, have it at the back of your mind that there are recommended dimensions - usually, Instagram posts are 1080p x 1080p. At the end of the day, if you are going to use stock images, then you might as well go all in and use their very best even if you have to put some bucks into it.

What About Content Planning?

We probably should have talked about this earlier on, but better late than never. Before you begin, anyway, you should ask yourself these two questions - what kind of content will fit your brand? and what is it that your audience wants to see? If you are able to find out the who, what and why of your Instagram brand, you will have taken a very important step for planning out your content strategy. If you have a heck of what your brand's about, and the sort of content your audience would prefer, you are ready to hone in and create the right type of posts from the onset.

When you find your branch niche and dedicate your efforts to just that, it will eventually pay off. A good number of Instagram accounts have gotten sidetracked because they were busy posting content that is not within their target audience and niche. If you do this, a slowed-down growth would actually be the least of your worries. Case in point, if you are a food business, you must plan your content in a way that it will be 100 percent based around gastronomy, and not about your selfies and vacations. The level of targeting, rather than going off the track of your brand niche, is quite essential if you want to grow that Instagram account as much as possible.

Once you have been able to answer those two questions, perhaps it is time to settle down and plan your content - usually weekly. How do we begin? Make a list of all the things that you will want to post on the page this week, if you are feeling extra organized, you can plan your content for the whole month. If you blog about fashion, for example, you may want to have about three outfit shots, and three-flat lays for the coming week that you can mix and match from. Of all the time-saving tips, one of the most important is to plan your photoshoots for a specific day and get content for many days' worth of Instagram posts. However you do it, just be intentional with your plan - always plan ahead, remember to be smart about.

For say Monday, you can take photos for your outfit's shots, and dedicate your time to flay lay the images on Friday. An Instagram entrepreneur should be able to batch his or her shoot together, as it does well to save plenty of time in the long run. You can also use this medium to scout for content and gather those that will be posted some weeks into the future. The bottom line is that the more organized you are with your time, the better the Instagram content you will be planning. At the end of the day, you will have a better chance of keeping your audience engaged all week and month long. Lastly, be intentional about your content planning all week long, as the life of your Instagram page pretty much depends on it.

Some tools to help out with content management on Instagram include Hootsuite, Combin, Later, Linktree, Boomerang and so on. These platforms for social media management help to make scheduling and publishing posts a piece of cake. You can use its Instagram options for scheduling your posts in advance, not having to worry about forgetting to publish them.

Pay Attention To Hashtags And Certain Accounts

In the Instagram game, hashtags are pretty important. There are certain accounts you should also follow in order to get the best kind of content to keep your fans engaged. In order to source great content to share, you sometimes need to brainstorm brands that you know have awe-inspiring Instagram content themselves, especially the ones whose audience is very similar to yours. It is best to look for the ones who are not direct competitors. To help with it, jot some of these ideas down in a notepad for reference purposes. Check out other Instagram accounts, after which you can make a list of those who whip up the best content you can give to your followers.

Starting from now, you need to begin following them in order for you to keep tabs with their recent posts and mode of sharing. While you do so, be vigilant about the specifics and save any posts you think are worthy of being shared by tapping on the bookmark icon below it, whether it's a write-up or video. You can as well create a separate collection where you can save the posts you intend reposting to your account anytime soon or later. What else can you do? Create a list of all the major hashtags that are relevant to your account. Search for these tags as they will help you discover associated content from other users. Hashtags can bring you the most visibility and engagement. They are not only a sensation on Instagram but also an all-round tool on nearly all the social media platforms, including Facebook and Twitter.

The next step is reaching out to the owners of the contents you have selected to get permission to share them on your platform. When you are able to locate a post you want to share with your followers, simply send the user a DM. But first, you can comment on the spot to let them know you have fallen in love with their Instagram content efforts and that you think your own followers will equally enjoy it. When contact is established, politely ask them for permission to share the content on your feed. Whatever you do, do not forget to let the user know that proper credit will be accorded to them. Most of the time, they will be happy and obliged to get more exposure, especially as they know you reckon that they are doing a great job.

Rather than sending a general private message, you can select the arrow symbol beneath each post to send it to the user to show them which post exactly you are interested in. Then, save the post to your feed - from Instagram's dashboard. Repost for Instagram takes the stress out of reposting photos and videos on your page while according credit to the original owner of the content. When you decide on what you want to report, simply copy the share URL and open repost. When you are in the app, you can position the watermark and send the reposted content back to Instagram. This method is actually more straightforward than the first, but bear in mind that the Repost app does not have the option of removing the watermark.

CHAPTER SEVEN

ALL ABOUT CAPTION

Caption. Think of your caption as the header in a magazine. The first few lines on every post, those are what captivate people to want to follow your page or to take any action that you want them to take. Under your caption, there is what is known as call-to-action. You don't expect people to do what is in your head; you have to mention it to them before they can do it. Followers need to be directed about what you want them to do. Tell a story with your profile and be consistent with it.

You may not be aware, but the importance of captioning is growing more than ever. To put things into perspective, there is an increasing number of ADA website lawsuits being filed against organizations that are failing to make provision for video captioning for people with disabilities such as visual or hearing impairments. This also includes other digital accommodations for blind, low vision, or other persons who have certain disabilities. If you are running one of those online organizations looking to avoid being sued, captioning is even all the more critical in all your business processes.

At this point, you may want to ask why the essentialness of caption is growing into something so important, perhaps because it was not so much of a big deal in the last decade. Well, here is another reason. Captioning is also growing due to several other reasons, which are as prevalent as the current litigation landscape. At least, for the fact that technology is changing, that video use and popularity are making significant strides, there is an all-cause for the rising relevance of captioning.

Caption Helps You Pass Messages Effectively

If your fans see a photo you posted on your Instagram page; they will want to know why or what the picture is about. When there is no caption for the image, then it becomes easy for people to form their own conclusions. It will make perfect sense to you why that photo exists, but that does not mean the reader thinks the same way you do. Because minds are always different and perceptions often conflicting, it is necessary to deliver a message fully by including an image caption. The caption will do well to yank the user from whatever sphere of thought they are in and make them specifically grab what it is you want them to understand.

When a caption is unavailable, it will be possible for the reader to look at your photo and easily form their own opinions. This can be turn out erroneous or counterproductive to what it is you want them to read, and that is not what you want. You need to be equipped well enough to control the situation and side in the caption. When you do this, you will be significantly removing any chances for misinterpretation, and that does a solid for your brand messaging. When your reader sees the pictures and reads the caption, then all is well that ends well. Any idea or opinion formed outside the complete package is totally the user's choice, and not your own doing. As the saying goes, I am responsible for what I say, not what you understand.

A Way To Educate And Create Curiosity

While trying to get a given message across with the aid of a caption, there are three ways you can do so. As bizarre as it may sound, the first strategy is to use a **problem**. The second is a **solution** while the third is a combo of the first two - **the problem-solution method**. One thing that is both common and interesting about these three methods is that they can create curiosity and anchor enlightenment.

The solution-only caption, which usually includes the product name helps give you a vivid guideline (or many guidelines) that enables you to see what is missing for yourself. It also lets you see what it is that you, as well as your users, can be missing both in the long and short runs. Ultimately, such captions on your Instagram page helps you take note of what's working in your sales copy.

Then, the problem-only caption helps you do a lot of things at the same time. If you want to know if your social media messaging is working as well as it should, this is the caption to use. If you want to get the hang of how presentation wakes up your audience, this is the caption to use. Rather than posting images that turn out controversial and somewhat misleading, it would be better to share them alongside some of society's most common problems.

Finally, there is the marrying of the problem and solution in one caption. Quick question: How do you know if your Instagram page business is working as well as you want it to? How will you be able to determine the level at which you are able to engage followers? Also, how are you able to know in advance that the way you are presenting your content is the right way to spark your audience alive? This approach will afford you clear guidelines that will equip you to see for yourself what's missing and what's working in your sales copy.

If you take a good look at these three methods of caption marketing, you will understand the extent to which they can generate curiosity and enlighten as much as possible. When people pick up their phones and navigate to your Instagram page, they intend to see something interesting, either they learn about new stuff or get motivated to go learn about them. Your social media handle needs to be that kind of platform people get that kind of value from. Asides quality, compelling images, and well-planned content, captions are the cream to the top of the Instagram package.

CONCLUSION

It's no news that social media brings in a lot of attention and emphasis when it comes to marketing your products and services. So, naturally, we think most brands should make it a priority to learn how to sell on Instagram. For a good reason. A presence on social media engages your followers, helps you find new customers, and contributes to your brand identity.

But, with all of those benefits aside, most people still get stuck on this one question: What's the return on investment? Is your time spent crafting strategies and creating posts quite literally paying off? What impact does this have on your business' bottom line?

Measuring the ROI of your social media efforts presents a challenge. But, make no mistake; you actually can leverage Instagram to close deals and make more sales. And, as the platform continues to evolve, the capabilities for selling are only going to grow. If you're apprehensive about learning how to sell on Instagram, don't be!

In terms of what's next? Well, it looks like Instagram will continue to become even more shop-able and e-commerce-driven. Instagram recently rolled out a payment feature to select users in the U.S. and the U.K. This allows users to store their payment information and make purchases—without ever leaving the Instagram app.

While the feature is starting out only with services—such as booking an appointment or a reservation—as opposed to actual products, we can only imagine that the latter isn't too far off into the future. Integration with Instagram's existing shoppable posts is more than likely in the works. Even more interesting? Instagram just recently announced plans to launch a stand-alone shopping app - make sure you know how to sell on Instagram before the official launch comes along.

So, without a doubt, e-commerce and ways that brands can leverage Instagram to increase sales are at the forefront of Instagram's mind— and it should be at the front of your mind too. Taking my business page into consideration, when we started Fabrics and Asoebi, the business was for a fabric sourcing company. There was this great media page called '*BellaNaijawedding*' with a lot of followers; the media page was about weddings and all. It occurred to me that if BellaNaija was to come into my niche and start sourcing fabrics, they would sell out because they already had a lot of people who are looking into getting married, looking for concepts of a dream wedding.

In terms of getting great content from your competitors or influencer, look at the number of followers, the number of likes on the post, and hashtags. Where I couldn't compete in terms of followers, I would compete in terms of captions and hashtags. You can use as much as 20 to 30 hashtags. One thing about hashtags, you will always get similar hashtags once you type it out, as Instagram will suggest other hashtags. So, with the right content, captions, and consistency, your account will grow. Once you start to see success, you will be motivated to do more. Once you get viral and big, it is easier to get bigger, with less stress.

Everything in this book won't work for you until you try it. So take action as soon as possible. Then, whatever you notice Instagram is promoting more, post them often. Right now, Instagram is promoting long-time videos known as 'Instagram tv.' This type of video will easily go viral. So you work more on them. So start as soon as possible and grow your organic followers before Instagram starts monetizing the process of making your post go viral, and you have to pay for ads. Take action starting from today!